Bird Homes

by Scott Shalaway

Contents

Bird Homes: Nesting & Roosting Space
Which birds use nest boxes?   2

The Hole Story
Why and how birds use nest boxes and natural cavities.   4

Nest Box Basics
Providing housing that birds need and prefer.   6

Predators & Parasites
How to baffle predators and fight parasites.   8

Questions & Answers
The most often-asked questions are answered.   12

Species Profiles of Cavity Nesters
A peek at the secret lives of birds.   16

Nest Box Specifications Chart
A reference for box size, hole size, mounting, and placement.   32

BILL THOMPSON, III

Front Cover: Carolina wren entering the nest box. Photograph by Maslowski Wildlife Productions.
Above: A male eastern bluebird at a nest box. Photograph by Bill Thompson, III.

A GUIDE TO BIRD HOMES was produced by the staff of *Bird Watcher's Digest*:
Publisher: Andy Thompson, Editor and Booklet Concept: Bill Thompson, III, Managing Editor: Jim Cirigliano, Booklet Design and Production: Claire Mullen

Bird Watcher's Digest is published by Pardson Corporation, P.O. Box 110, Marietta, Ohio 45750. To order additional copies of *A GUIDE TO BIRD HOMES*, or our other booklets, *A GUIDE TO BACKYARD BIRDS, ENJOYING PURPLE MARTINS MORE, ENJOYING BLUEBIRDS MORE, ENJOYING HUMMINGBIRDS MORE,* and *ENJOYING BIRD FEEDING MORE*, or for *BWD* subscription information, call us toll-free, at 1-800-879-2473.
ISBN # 1-880241-07-2

Bird

Homes

Chickadees, titmice, bluebirds, and wrens. Nuthatches, woodpeckers, tree swallows, and violet-green swallows. Kestrels, screech-owls, and wood ducks. The common bond these diverse birds share is the habit of nesting in cavities.

Which birds use nest boxes?

Nature provides cavities in a variety of ways. An ice storm breaks a limb off a tree or a bolt of lightning splits a tree trunk, leaving behind an open wound. Fungi invade the injury. Over time, the heartwood rots. Eventually a cavity-nesting bird claims the hole, perhaps a great crested flycatcher, a saw-whet owl, or a pygmy nuthatch.

Woodpeckers create most new cavities. They excavate new holes every year as part of their breeding behavior. Because woodpeckers create their own cavities, ornithologists call them primary cavity nesters. The ecological result is a steady supply of once-used cavities for secondary cavity nesters—such as wrens, bluebirds, flycatchers, and swallows—that rely on pre-existing holes.

ROBERTMCCAW.COM

At left: Western bluebirds establish residence in a suitable nest box.

Above: Purple martins during nest building.

Due to the effects of high winds, ice damage, insects, fungi, and a variety of plant diseases, there's never a shortage of dead, cavity-bearing trees. But because most people fail to see any value in them, such trees tend not to stand very long. One significant ecological consequence is that many cavity-nesting birds find it difficult to locate suitable nesting cavities. For decades wildlife biologists, ornithologists, and bird watchers have addressed this critical habitat shortage by providing and promoting the use of artificial nest sites—

MASLOWSKI WILDLIFE PRODUCTIONS

which most of us call nest boxes or birdhouses.

The use of nest boxes by birds is a remarkable conservation success story. Most cavity-nesting birds are common and require only suitable nest sites to maintain stable populations. Without cavities, their populations decline and may eventually disappear. Add properly maintained artificial nest sites—nest boxes—and their populations rebound.

The recovery of bluebird populations is a classic example of the impact of nest boxes. By the 1940s and 50s, all three bluebird species had been decimated by pesticide use and habitat destruction. The birds disappeared from many parts of their traditional range.

Thanks to the dedicated efforts of bluebird conservationists who promoted the use of nest boxes for bluebirds, trails of nest boxes appeared around the country. Though the pioneers of bluebird conservation are too numerous to mention, T.E. Musselman is credited with originating the bluebird trail concept. Lawrence Zeleny popularized it with his 1976 book, *The Bluebird: How You Can Help Its Fight for Survival*. Along the way, other cavity-nesting birds reaped the benefits of these new nest sites. Chickadees, titmice, wrens, and swallows used artificial cavities as eagerly as bluebirds.

In just 20 years, bluebirds rebounded from drastically reduced numbers to almost common status in many parts of the country. Since 1981, I have placed trails of nest boxes in Oklahoma, West Virginia, and Pennsylvania, and at each site bluebirds used the boxes within the first two years. Providing nest boxes is the easiest and most effective act an individual can perform to encourage cavity-nesting birds.

Nest boxes have also played an important role in restoring the wood duck. Overhunting and habitat

The Hole Story

I in North America only about 85 of our 650 breeding birds use cavities for nesting or roosting. Cavities offer much more security than the open nests of birds such as robins and doves. So why do so few birds use cavities for nesting? Here's the "hole" story.

It seems logical that, compared to an open nest, a cavity should provide better protection from the elements and predators for both the nestlings and the incubating adults. Cavities are well protected from rain and insulated from late spring freezes and mid-summer heat. Crows and jays—major predators on birds' nests—are usually foiled by the small entrance hole. Furthermore, cavity nesters are rarely victims of cowbird parasitism.

But does this protection translate to higher nesting success? The answer is yes. If success is measured as the percentage of nests that fledge at least one young bird, nesting success is much higher in cavities than in open nests. Nesting studies have shown that 60 to 80 percent of cavity nests succeed, while only 20 to 40 percent of open nests are successful.

Cavity nesters take advantage of the security cavities provide by extend-

Tree swallows often use large goose or chicken feathers in their nest construction.

Below: A red-headed woodpecker excavating a nest.

destruction once threatened woodies with extinction. Stricter hunting regulations, habitat protection, and the use of artificial cavities rescued them. Today wood ducks are one of North America's more common ducks.

The purpose of this booklet is to provide the information necessary to turn an active backyard bird watcher into a responsible nest-box landlord. Bluebirds and purple martins are not the only birds that use human-supplied housing, though these popu-

lar species get most of the attention.

When I began studying cavity nesters, bluebirds and purple martins were my primary subjects. Over the years, hundreds have fledged from nest boxes I have provided and monitored. But along the way I became enamored with the less glamorous cavity nesters—wrens, swallows, flycatchers, chickadees, titmice, and others. I hope this booklet will convince you that these cavity nesters deserve your attention and assistance as well. 🔻

ing the brood-rearing period. Nestling bluebirds, chickadees, and wrens, for example, remain in the nest for 16 to 22 days. Compare this to a nestling period of just 9 to 11 days for open-nesting species such as cardinals and catbirds. The extra time in the nest permits young birds to leave the cavity bigger, stronger, and better able to fly than their open-nesting counterparts.

If cavities are such great places to nest, then why don't all birds use them? Birds require certain physical skills and behaviors to use cavities. Cavity nesters must have strong feet that can cling to the vertical face of a tree or nest box. Furthermore, a bird must

be curious and fearless about exploring dark holes and crevices. Virtually all cavity nesters possess these traits. Species adapted for nesting in the open do not.

Because suitable cavities are almost always in short supply, there are usually more pairs of cavity nesters than cavities. This leads to fierce competition. That's why it's so easy to get cavity nesters to use nest boxes placed in suitable habitat.

The bottom line is that cavities are great places to nest, but because they are a limited resource, only relatively few species are adapted to take advantage of them. 🔻

Nest Box Basics

Whether you buy your nest boxes at a store or nature center, or build them from scratch, there are certain characteristics your housing should have to best suit the needs of nesting birds. Here are some recommendations for nest box basics:

• The lumber used should be untreated and at least ¾-inch thick to protect nests from spring chills and summer heat. Exterior plywood, cedar, and pine work well.

• Do not paint or stain the inside of the box. If you paint or stain the outside of the box, use a light earth tone color so sunlight and heat will be reflected, not absorbed.

• Use galvanized screws to assemble the nest box. It will last years longer than one built with nails or with glue, which will rapidly disintegrate as the wood warps and shrinks.

Proper house construction (left) and careful monitoring (right) are two ways to provide your birds with a healthier environment.

JULIE ZICKEFOOSE

• Your access to the inside of the nest box should be easy for nest inspections and box maintenance. The best box designs feature a side or front panel that can be swung up or out to gain access to the inside.

• Perches on the front of a nest box are not necessary. All cavity nesters have strong feet and can easily cling to vertical wooden surfaces. Perches only give easy access to house sparrows, starlings, and predators.

• The roof of the nest box should extend well over the entrance hole to protect the opening from driving rain and predators.

• The inside front panel of the box should be deeply scored below the hole to give emerging birds a ladder for exiting the box.

• The floor of the nest box should have at least four ⅜-inch drain holes so the box can drain if it does get wet. The floor should be recessed (as shown at left) so that no end grain is exposed to soak up water in wet weather.

• Ventilation holes near the top allow excess heat to escape. Plug holes with weather-stripping putty in cold weather.

• The nest box should be protected from predators. The best way to protect your nest boxes is to mount them on poles with a predator baffle in place below the box. (See the baffle design on page 10 of this booklet.)

Housing Placement

Once you have acquired housing, you need to place it in the right habitat. Use the information in the species profiles section of this booklet to learn more about the birds you hope to attract, and

BILL THOMPSON, III

use the nest box reference chart at the end of the booklet for habitat specifics.

Having selected a spot within appropriate habitat, make certain your nest boxes are securely mounted and baffled against predators (more about this topic later). Some species, such as martins and swallows, also require a clear flight path to and from the hole entrance.

Looking into a Nest Box

You slowly open a nest box and see a black-capped chickadee sitting on its nest. What do you do? Simply close the box, walk away, and record in your notebook that the female was on the nest, probably incubating eggs.

This scenario underscores the reason nest boxes should be easy to open from the front or side. Spending several minutes disassembling a nest box to check its contents can be enough to drive a nesting bird away permanently.

If the female leaves as you approach, or as you open the box, inspect the nest quickly, record your findings, and leave the area. Your complete visit should take no more than 30 seconds. If you are able to keep your visit this brief, the female will return to the nest box shortly. You may even want to watch from about 30 yards away and time how long it takes for her to return to the nest. After the eggs

hatch and the parents are bringing food to the chicks every few minutes, you may also want to record their comings and goings.

If you know the species using your nest box, check the species profile (beginning on page 17 of this booklet) for information about its incubation period. If you know the approximate date egg-laying ended and incubation began, you can estimate the hatching date of the eggs. This is important information. Timing is everything for a nest-box landlord. If you visit the nest during incubation or late in the nestling stage, you may cause nest abandonment or premature fledging. A good general rule is to limit nest box visits to the 10 days immediately after hatching. Resist the urge to visit nestlings—appealing as they may be— more often than necessary.

Monitoring Your Nest Boxes

Observing and recording the progress of active nests is perhaps the most fascinating aspect of being a landlord to cavity nesting birds. For most of the nesting season, a weekly visit to each box will provide an accurate snapshot of the lives of your birds, without undue disturbance.

Recording Your Observations

Here's how to record your observations: Devote a separate field notebook to your nest boxes, allowing several pages per nest box. Record what you see during your nest box inspections. Include the following information: Is the box being used? By what species? Has courtship or nest building begun? If there is a nest in the box, what is it made of? If there are eggs, how many and what do they look like? ✒

Predators &

They can slither, fly, climb, and jump.

Nest boxes that are baffled against predators result in higher nesting success for birds.

BILL THOMPSON, III

Parasites
And they want your birds.

After your nest boxes have fledged a few broods and you learn about the nesting cycle firsthand, you will feel both proud and protective. If you lose a nest to predators, you will feel violated and will want to make your nest boxes safer. Making nest boxes predator-proof is not easy, but there are several ways to make things difficult for predators hungry for your birds.

The first rule for defeating predators is to eliminate their access to the nest box. For pole-mounted housing placed out in the open, this is easily accomplished with a stovepipe or cylindrical baffle.

Not all cavity nesters will accept housing placed in the middle of a yard or meadow, away from the protective cover of the woods and underbrush. For woodland and edge-nesting species such as woodpeckers, nuthatches, and screech-owls, it is sometimes best (and most convenient for the landlord) if the nest box is mounted on a tree. In this case you should examine the feasibility of attaching a two-foot length of aluminum or galvanized metal flashing to the tree trunk. This will inhibit—but not eliminate—access by snakes, raccoons, and other predators. Larger boxes can sometimes be fitted with a hole extender—a square, open-ended box, about 4 inches by 4 inches, that fits over the hole. It allows the nesting birds access, but keeps raccoons from reaching in. Cylindrical hole-mounted guards are available commercially for use on nest boxes for bluebirds and swallows.

Box-mounted Guards

A box-mounted predator guard is a ¾-inch thickness of wood, fitted over the entrance hole, that increases the distance across which a raccoon or cat must reach to grab the nest contents. These guards are only marginally effective against mammalian predators—a raccoon will often chew them off—and they do nothing to stop climbing snakes. More elaborate hole-mounted guards must be mounted after eggs have been laid (note: mounting these baffles sometimes causes nest abandonment in skittish birds). Clearly, hole-mounted predator guards leave something to be desired.

Pole-mounted Baffles

The most effective antipredator strategy is to rig a baffle on the mounting pole below the nest box. This baffle might be a commercially purchased metal cylinder, or it could be a homemade sheet metal skirt. In any case, protection from below is essential to deter snakes, raccoons, and other climbing predators. Perhaps the most effective and easily made predator baffle design currently available is the one shown on page 10. It was originally designed by Virginia bluebird landlord Ron Kingston. Landlords using this baffle have reported tremendous success in eliminating predation at their nest boxes.

When thinking about baffling your

How to Make the Gilbertson Baffle & Pole Mount

Materials used: aluminum electrical conduit ½'' diameter x 5' long, #4 iron rebar ½'' x 5' long, two ½'' conduit connectors, two ¾'' machine screws (flat head), ½'' strapping brackets and weatherproof screws (to mount box to pole), duct tape, hanger iron (in two 7'' strips), two machine screws with nuts for hanger iron, galvanized stovepipe (34'' x 7'') with 7'' steel cap, and a knockout punch for ½'' conduit (hole .89 ½'') to make a neat hole in the stovepipe cap to accommodate the pipe.

Buy ½'' aluminum electrical conduit and ½'' iron rebar in a 10' length and have it cut at the store or cut it with a hacksaw into two 5' lengths. This will make two pole setups. With a mallet, drive one 5' length of iron rebar halfway into the ground. Slip one 5' length of conduit over the rebar; the rebar serves to support the conduit. Drop a ½'' conduit connector over the top of the rebar, and replace the lower screw in it with a ¾'' machine screw. This connector serves as a sleeve to affix the conduit firmly in its supporting rebar, and it prevents swiveling. Tighten both screws down—the lower screw into the rebar and the top screw into the conduit.

Using the knockout punch, make a hole in the center of the stovepipe cap. Bend and crimp the stovepipe into a cylinder. Fit the cap into the knurled end of the stovepipe.

Hold box up at height it will be mounted. A few inches beneath the box, run a double strip of duct tape around the conduit pipe. Bolt the two strips of hanger iron securely around the duct tape, on either side of the mounting pipe, and bend them as shown. Slip the assembled baffle over the top of the pipe and down to support the hardware cloth. Duct tape wrapped around the pole helps hold the hanger iron in place. Slip the assembled baffle over the hanger iron bracket, just below where the nest box will hang (the higher on the pole, the better). It should wobble a little, which further discourages climbing predators. Now mount the nest box using the strapping brackets. You're done!

A bird's-eye-view of a raccoon and the stovepipe baffle mount. The slick metal baffle wobbles on the pole, preventing snakes and climbing animals from reaching the box. Baffle pole and mount designed by Steve Gilbertson, whose sparrow-resistant PVC and wooden Gilbertson boxes mount without hardware on ½'' electrical conduit. Boxes are sold by the case of 14. Call Steve Gilbertson, 35900 Dove Street, Aitkin, MN 56431 • (218-927-1953.) Thanks to Ron Kingston for his original baffle design.

boxes, remember to think like a predator. If you can imagine gaining access to your nest boxes, an actual predator can likely do so quite easily.

If you put nest boxes out without baffling them in some way you are probably doing little, over the long run, to help your birds, but you might be helping predators to an easy meal.

Parasites

Few nests in boxes, or even those in natural cavities, escape infestation by parasites. The most common nest parasites are blowflies, mites, and lice. Depending on the degree of infestation these parasites can be an annoyance or a deadly problem for the birds.

Blowfly larvae are among the most serious pests. These maggotlike larvae attach themselves to nestlings' feet and wings and suck blood from the chicks. Heavy infestations can slow the growth rate of nestlings and sometimes even kill them. Look for whitish maggots or brown pupal capsules that look like coffee beans in the bottom of a nestbox, in the lower third of the nesting material.

Lice and mites will appear as barely visible, moving, grayish specks on the nestlings and nesting material.

If you regularly monitor your nest boxes you will be able to detect the presence of these parasites.

NEVER use pesticides—even in small amounts—in or around a nestbox.

In the event of a heavy parasite infestation, remove the nestlings from the nest, and place them temporarily in a grass-lined bucket. Remove the old nest from the box and sweep out the bottom of the box. Fashion a new nest from grasses and the appropriate nesting material and replace the nestlings in the new nest. This should reduce the pests enough to allow the nestlings to fledge.

After all the birds have fledged, remove the nesting material and wash the inside of the box with a solution of water (8 parts) and bleach (1 part). Rinse thoroughly and allow to dry before closing the box.

Other Insect Pests

Sometimes wasps, bees, and ants move into nest boxes, and may even exclude birds. To discourage wasps and bees from nesting in your boxes, rub liquid soap, or a light coating of petroleum jelly, on the inside roof of the nestbox. Be sure to keep the soap away from areas that the birds will contact. To reduce ant access to boxes, use Teflon tape and/ or Teflon spray on the mounting pole and baffle. Axle grease and products like tanglefoot do not always work, and, more importantly, can harm birds.

For persistent insect problems, move the nest boxes to a new location, after the birds fledge. ❧

ROBERTMCCAW.COM

Unprotected boxes mounted on fence posts can be easy targets for snakes and raccoons.

Questions
& Answers

Who, what, where, when, why, and how.

As new people discover the joys and challenges of providing nest boxes for cavity nesters, the same questions come up every year. Here are answers to many of the most frequently asked questions.

Q: When do cavity nesters begin using their nest boxes?

A: Breeding behavior for many cavity nesters begins as early as January or February in warmer southern and western regions. In Oklahoma, for example, I always had a few bluebird and chickadee clutches in March, but in northern West Virginia I rarely see any eggs before mid-April.

Nest boxes should be erected in suitable habitat in January (even earlier for screech-owls). Non-migratory cavity nesters such as nuthatches, chickadees, and titmice investigate potential nest sites throughout the winter and are ready to nest as soon as springlike weather arrives.

On the other hand, it's never too late. I've put up new boxes in mid-June and have had bluebirds or wrens move in within 24 hours. Nest box use is usually a result of supply and demand.

Be patient. Most boxes are not used the first year they are erected. It may take two or three years for birds

to accept a nest box as part of the natural scene.

Q: How often should I check my nest boxes?

A: Start checking nest boxes a few days after you see birds carrying nesting material to the box. In southern states this may be as early as February; in northern areas it may be mid-to-late April.

During the nest-building stage, you may check boxes every day or two. During the egg-laying stage, you may check nests every few days. This is a good time to check clutch size. The female generally lays one egg each day, usually in the morning. This takes only a few minutes. The female may spend the rest of the day away from the box foraging, so checking boxes at this time does not usually disturb the parents.

Don't disturb boxes at all during incubation. Three days after the eggs hatch, you may again check boxes every few days. In all cases, if possible, check the box when the parents are away from the nest gathering food.

Q: Does checking boxes disturb the birds or cause them to abandon the nest?

A: My experience indicates that the most critical time during nesting is incubation. Avoid disturbing an incubating bird, or it may abandon the nest.

Incubation in small cavity nesters such as chickadees, bluebirds, and wrens takes about 14 days. During the first 10 days of incubation birds are particularly sensitive to disturbance. During the last few days, adults sit tightly or actively defend the nest when an intruder visits. Their investment in time and energy at this point is so great that they will do whatever it takes to hatch the eggs.

After the eggs hatch, give the chicks two or three days before checking them again. During the first few days after hatching, one of the adults usually broods the chicks to keep them warm, especially on cold, damp days. Never risk subjecting young birds to cold weather.

Later, as chicks become feathered, you should resist the temptation to continue checking the nest. Disturbances late in the nesting cycle may cause some nestlings to fledge prematurely. Those that leave the nest before they are ready are unlikely to survive.

Q: How do I actually go about checking a box?

A: Assuming you know what is in the box (more about surprises later), walk briskly and directly to the box. Place one hand over the hole. Next, swing the door open just enough to peek inside. If no adult is present, swing the door completely open, take notes, close the door, and leave as quickly as possible.

If an adult is on the nest, close the door carefully, and keep your hand over the hole for about 30 seconds. Then quickly walk away. Most of the time the adult will stay on the nest.

Simply checking the contents of a box should take no more than 30 sec-

onds. This is why nest boxes must be easy to open, preferably from the front or side.

Q: What kinds of information should I record?

A: Before opening the box, record the date and note any behavior related to the box. Wrens, for example, often fly to within inches of my face and scold when I check their boxes.

After opening the box, examine the nest. Identify it, using the east or west edition of Hal Harrison's *Field Guide to Birds' Nests* (from the Peterson series). If you can't identify the nest, watch the box closely until an adult returns.

Note the materials from which the nest is made. Look for interesting nesting materials such as moss, feathers, string, or plastic wrappers. Every tufted titmouse nest I've ever seen, for example, has contained a shed snakeskin, and white-breasted nuthatches build their nests on a foundation of small bark chips. A foundation of twigs indicates wrens, a mossy base suggests chickadees, and a simple cup of dry grass or pine needles identifies bluebird nests.

Record the number of eggs or chicks. It is often helpful to photograph the contents of the box for future reference.

During the course of the nesting period try to time your visits to determine the following: clutch size (number of eggs), hatching date, hatching success (percent of eggs hatched), and fledging success (percent of nestlings that leave the nest).

If predators destroy a nest, note the nest's appearance and look for clues that might identify the predator. Snakes, for instance, eat eggs whole, so they're often responsible when eggs vanish from an apparently undisturbed nest.

Keep your nest boxes up all year long. During very cold winter weather many birds sleep in cavities to conserve body heat. Bluebirds and nuthatches don't mind a crowd; sometimes 10 or 12 individuals cram into a cavity for the night.

Raccoons, on the other hand, usually reach in, pulling much of the nest out as they grope for eggs or chicks. Also note the presence of parasites.

Observations such as these enable amateurs to make valuable contributions to ornithology. *Sialia*, the quarterly journal of the North American Bluebird Society, for example, relies heavily on contributions from volunteer landlords who are willing to share their recorded nest box results with others.

Q: What shall I do with my results?

A: There are many applications and uses for your records. Keep them for your own enjoyment and reference. Make year-to-year comparisons. Present your findings to the local bird or garden club. Summarize your results in writing, and submit them to your state ornithological society. Use your results to get others interested in cavity nesters and nest boxes. Your only limits are your own energy and imagination.

Q: What should I do if I find a house sparrow or starling nest in one of my boxes?

A: These two non-native species are pests, and a serious threat to native cavity nesters. Both species are extremely aggressive when competing for a nest site. Not only do they take over nest boxes used by native species, but sometimes they actually kill the occupants and may even incorporate

the remains into their own nests.

Starlings can be excluded with a 1½-inch entrance hole, which will still admit all cavity nesters except great crested flycatchers and the large woodpeckers. Discouraging house sparrows is more difficult. When either of these species occupies a box, there are two primary methods of control. The first involves daily removal of any nesting material and nest contents. If you keep this effort up, the sparrows or starlings will likely abandon the site, and will look elsewhere to nest. However a nest-removal program does not always discourage these birds, so a more permanent control method may be necessary.

If you wish to remove problem birds permanently, approach the nest box shortly after dark, cover the hole, and remove the incubating bird. Kill it quickly and humanely (neither species is protected by any state or federal law), and remove the nest and destroy its contents. This advice may seem cold and cruel, but it may be necessary to keep boxes free for native species.

One way to avoid having to take such measures is to avoid placing your nest boxes in areas where starlings and house sparrows abound, such as near livestock feeding areas, in city parks, and near shopping malls, where lots of human activity supports these birds.

Q: Am I likely to encounter any surprises while checking boxes?

A: Yes. Be careful. Paper wasps build nests in bird boxes. I knock them out with a long stick and crush them.

Occasionally a snake gets into a box and devours its contents. The snake will do you no harm, except perhaps to alarm you when you open the box. In some parts of the country venomous copperheads venture into nest boxes. Always consider this possibility before opening a nest box.

I don't kill snakes I find in boxes, and I urge you not to, either. Snakes have their place in the natural order of things. Still, it is best to baffle your nest boxes to prevent any unpleasant surprises for you, or for the birds.

Finally, be careful if you find a box full of white-footed mice or flying squirrels. These mammals sometimes bite when frightened and they can deliver a pretty good nip. I pull out mouse nests but leave the flying squirrels undisturbed (I've got a soft spot for flying squirrels.) Evicted mice simply scamper to a nearby underground burrow that they maintain for just such emergencies.

Q: Should old nests be removed from nest boxes?

A: For years the answer to this question was an emphatic yes. Biologists argued that used nests harbor parasites that can infest subsequent broods of nestlings.

Recent research, however, suggests that when given a choice, bluebirds and other cavity nesters often choose a nest box that contains an old nest instead of an empty box. Apparently, a tiny parasitic wasp that controls blowfly populations lives and over-winters in old nests. Nests built on top of old nests may be more likely to succeed because the parasitic wasps are present and effectively control the blowflies. More field work is needed to confirm this hypothesis. You may wish to conduct your own trials. Just remember to monitor nestlings for blowfly infestations. (See "Predators & Parasites" beginning on page 8 of this booklet.)

Q: Are there any places I shouldn't put up nest boxes?

A: Boxes near barns and feedlots attract house sparrows, so it's best to keep boxes at least 100 yards away from these areas. Also, boxes placed more than a few yards inside the perimeter of a woodlot attract squirrels and porcupines. These rodents love to chew nest boxes. Placing nest boxes in areas of heavy pesticide use is not good for the birds. And if you have a cat which kills birds, it's best not to lure birds into areas where your cat might get them.

Q: Do birds use nest boxes for anything other than nesting ?

A: During very cold winter weather many birds sleep in cavities to conserve body heat. This is a powerful argument for keeping nest boxes up all year long. Bluebirds and nuthatches don't mind a crowd; sometimes 10 or 12 individuals cram into a cavity for the night. Chickadees and woodpeckers are more likely to roost singly.

Screech-owls use cavities throughout the year for a variety of purposes, including eating, prey caching, roosting, and breeding. A pair of screech-owls may require as many as five cavities or nest boxes per year. ✒

Species

Profiles

Providing nesting and roosting space for birds requires some knowledge of the birds themselves, their nesting cycles, and habitat preferences. In this chapter you'll learn about the different families of cavity nesting birds.

An overview of the nesting cycles of cavity nesters.

Chickadees

Chickadees are among the most widely distributed birds in North America. No matter where you live in North America, you've probably got chickadees nesting nearby. **Black-capped chickadees** occupy the northern half of the United States and the southern half of Canada, and range all the way to Alaska. **Boreal chickadees** range across Canada's northern tier. **Carolina chickadees** occupy the southeastern portion of the United States. **Mountain chickadees** inhabit most of the mountainous areas west of the Great Plains. And **chestnut-backed chickadees** are found along the West Coast of North America.

Chickadees inhabit forests and forest edges, where they actively seek caterpillars, spiders, egg cases, and other protein-rich food during the breeding season, switching their diet to seeds, fruit, and nuts in the fall and winter months.

BILL THOMPSON, III

Although chickadees have stout, strong bills and can excavate their own cavities in rotten wood, they often use natural cavities, old woodpecker holes, and nest boxes. Most of my experience has been with Carolina and black-capped chickadees, but the nesting biology is similar for all species of chickadees.

Chickadees produce only one brood, although they will renest if their first nest is destroyed by weather or predators. Chickadee nests are fairly easy to identify—neat fur-lined cups embedded in a thick foundation of dry green moss. Clutch size varies from 4 to 10 eggs. The female incubates the clutch for 12 or 13 days. The largest chickadee clutch I've ever found was on a golf course in Wheeling, West Virginia—nine eggs by a pair

At left: Carolina chickadee parents feed their young at the nest right up until fledging.
Above: A tufted titmouse takes alpaca wool for use as nesting material.

CONNIE TOOPS

of Carolina chickadees. All nine eggs hatched, and all nine nestlings fledged.

Titmice

Five species of titmice occur in North America, but their distribution is more restricted than that of the chickadees. The **tufted titmouse** occurs throughout the eastern United States to the central Great Plains. The closely-related **black-crested titmouse** occurs in the southern Great Plains and south into Mexico. The **juniper titmouse** inhabits the southwestern United States. The **bridled titmouse's** range extends from southern Arizona and New Mexico, south into Mexico. The tiny **oak titmouse** occurs farthest west, inhabiting much of California to the Pacific Coast.

Like chickadees, titmice live in mixed woodlands and forest edges. Unlike chickadees, titmice do not excavate their own cavities; they rely on old woodpecker holes, natural cavities, and nest boxes. Within their range, tufted titmice can be easy to attract to nest boxes that are offered in or near woodland edges.

Titmouse nests contain more dried leaves and less moss than chickadee nests, though the cup itself is lined with animal fur. Consequently, titmouse nests appear messy. During the egg-laying and incubation periods, the female titmouse covers the eggs with nesting material when she leaves the nest, presumably to hide them from unwelcome visitors. Clutch size ranges from 4 to 8 eggs; the female incubates the eggs for about two weeks.

Titmice are resourceful when searching for nesting materials. I was in the woods early one morning when I happened to watch a pair of tufted titmice gathering nesting material from an unusual source.

As I walked along, I noticed a raccoon sleeping high in the crotch of a large beech tree. Soon two titmice approached and perched near the raccoon.

By now the raccoon was descending the beech headfirst. Suddenly the female titmouse darted for the raccoon's ringed tail. Hovering for just an instant, she plucked a bunch of hair from the tail. Over the next two minutes she made the daring move four more times, always careful to stay away from the raccoon's head.

Using my binoculars, I followed the female titmouse as she flew to another beech tree. She entered a small hole about 20 feet above the ground. In a few weeks her chicks would enjoy the bird world's version of flannel sheets.

Birds often use mammal hair as nesting material. It insulates the nest just as it did the original owner's body. Usually, however, the fur is stripped from a carcass, such as a road-killed mammal. I once tested the appeal of carcass fur by placing a road-killed opossum in my backyard. Sure enough, a parade of titmice, chickadees, and nuthatches visited the carcass repeatedly and departed with puffballs of fur.

Nuthatches

The nuthatches are known by many as the "upside-down birds." They scoot headfirst down the trunks of trees as easily as woodpeckers hitch their way upward. At feeders, nuthatches often hang upside-down to reach favorite foods. They open seeds and nuts by wedging them in bark crevices and then hacking open the seed. ("Hatch" is a corruption of "hack.")

Four species of nuthatches occupy the forests of North America. The **white-breasted nuthatch** is a widespread, permanent resident of most of the forested areas of the United States and southern Canada. White-breasted nuthatches are most visible during winter, when, on leafless trees, they are easily spotted as they work their way down and around the tree trunks. They are small, handsome birds. Only five inches long, they have a white breast and face with a blue-gray back and a black cap and neck. Females resemble males, but their caps are a duller slate gray.

White-breasted nuthatches regularly visit backyard feeders, but they don't normally travel in feeding flocks, like chickadees, titmice, and goldfinches. A single pair visits my yard each morning. And even when I can't see the birds, I can hear their distinctive nasal *ank, ank, ank* call.

Adults maintain a loose pair bond even during the winter months, often traveling alone, but within earshot of each other. At night each bird roosts alone in its own tree cavity. On extremely cold nights, several nuthatches may roost together.

This male white-breasted nuthatch is bringing food back to the nest.

In March or April, the female finds a new cavity in which to build a nest and lay her eggs. The base of the nest consists of small chips of bark, each about an inch square. The nest cup is lined with animal fur. Both parents incubate the clutch of 5 to 10 eggs for 12 days. Young white-breasted nuthatches fledge when they are about three weeks old.

Red-breasted nuthatches nest in coniferous forests in Canada, the Rocky Mountains, and in the north-central and northeastern United States. Unlike other nuthatches, red-breasteds migrate for the winter, but they stay within the continental United States, where they often visit backyard feeders. Red-breasted nuthatches are distinguished from the white-breasteds by their smaller size, rusty bellies, and a striking black eyeline topped by a white eyebrow stripe.

Red-breasted nuthatches lay 4 to 9 eggs, and the female incubates them for 15 or 16 days. The young fledge about three weeks after hatching.

Brown-headed nuthatches are familiar residents of pine woodlands in the southeastern states. Though their brown cap is distinctive, this nuthatch is also easy to recognize by sound: its high-pitched, doubled-noted call sounds just like a squeaky rubber duck.

Both sexes share incubation of 3 to 9 eggs for about two weeks. The young leave the nest when they are about 18 days old. Occasionally an unmated, young male serves as an extra helper at the nest.

Pygmy nuthatches are the western equivalent of the brown-headed nuthatch. They are quite similar in appearance, except for the pygmy's grayish cap. The female incubates a clutch of 6 to 8 eggs for about 15 days. Young fledge at about three weeks of age. The breeding unit of the pygmy nuthatch consists of up to five birds—the breeding pair and as many as three nest helpers. Research has shown that pairs with nest helpers usually fledge more young than those without helpers.

Wrens

Of all the cavity-nesting birds, wrens are the most tolerant of human beings. Perhaps "enamored" would be a better word. Wrens can't seem to get close enough to us. I've had wrens nest in my garage, on my back porch in a clothespin bag, and in an exhaust fan vent tube. The wrens almost always ignore the eight nest boxes within 50 yards of our house.

Wren nests are easy to recognize when found in a nest box, or anywhere else. Invariably the base of the nest consists of twigs. Often these twigs fill the box and even stick out of the hole. The cup is lined with grass, rootlets, moss, leaves, animal fur, snakeskins, and usually some feathers.

We once had a **house wren** that nested in our clothespin bag. Before any eggs were laid, I removed the bag. The wrens reacted almost immediately. When they discovered the bag was gone, they came to the window on the back-porch door and began scolding and pecking on the glass. They wanted their nest back. After removing some clothespins, I returned the bag to its hook on the porch. Within minutes the wrens returned and began building a new nest.

Reports abound of house wrens nesting in flower pots, mailboxes, tin cans, outhouses, old sneakers, and of course, clothespin bags. The pair nesting in the bathroom fan vent tube was a first for me, though. For several weeks I eavesdropped on the begging nestlings every time the adults entered the vent with food.

House wrens are the most widespread of the wrens found in the United States. Their range reaches well into Canada, and as far south as Chile. They live in brushy old fields, shrubby backyards, and forest edges. They often are the first tenants to occupy a backyard birdhouse.

Drab and brown, house wrens make up for their dull appearance with an explosive, bubbly song. A house wren's predawn chorus rings like an alarm clock that can't be shut off.

House wrens usually attempt their first nest shortly after returning in the spring. Males arrive first, establish their territories, then begin the business of nest building. They busily fill almost every available cavity with twigs. When females arrive about a week later, pairing occurs and the female then chooses one of her mate's offerings. After choosing one of the "dummy" nests, the female lines the cup and begins to lay eggs at the rate of one per day.

Other cavity nesters usually ignore boxes with unused "dummy" nests because the boxes are so crammed with twigs that there is no room for another nest. That's why it is a good idea to clean dummy nests out of the other nest boxes after the female wren has chosen a box and begun incubating her eggs.

The female house wren lays 6 to 8

Carolina wrens will nest in many human-made objects, even near residences.

eggs and incubates them for 13 days. The male brings food to her while she incubates. After the eggs hatch, both parents feed the nestlings. Young remain in the nest for about 17 days. Two broods per year are common in house wrens; some birds manage three.

Since they often claim ownership of every cavity in their territory, house wrens sometimes harass other cavity nesters until they abandon their nests. Occasionally they even puncture the eggs of others in their quest to claim a cavity or nest box. Bluebirds, swallows, chickadees, and titmice are frequent targets of these assaults. There are many records of "vindictive" house wrens. If their own nest is destroyed by a predator or by human intervention, they will often despoil the nearby nests of other birds. If house wrens are nesting in one of your nest boxes, do not evict them or destroy their nest, even if the box was intended for another species.

Carolina wrens are much more handsome than the mouse-brown house wren. Carolinas are a rich, rusty-brown above and have a bold white eye stripe. Their song is a loud, easy-to-learn series of triplet whistles: *teakettle, teakettle, teakettle!*

Carolina wrens are nonmigratory birds with a range that stretches from central Texas, north to near Chicago, and east to northern Massachusetts.

Carolina wrens usually nest in a wide variety of nooks and crannies, rather than in nest boxes. For the last few years, a pair has nested in a can of nails in my garage. Clutch size averages 5 or 6 eggs, and the female incubates the eggs for about 14 days. The young fledge when they are about two weeks old. Carolina wrens typically raise two broods in a breeding season.

The third wren that commonly

uses nest boxes is the **Bewick's wren**. Its historical range extends across the southern half of the United States, but its numbers are inexplicably down in the Southeast. In the western parts of its range, the Bewick's wren is still fairly common.

Bewick's wrens lay 5 to 8 eggs; the female incubates them for 14 days. Young fledge at about two weeks of age. Two broods are typical for this wren. Cowbird parasitism is rare among cavity nesters, but I recorded it three times in Bewick's wren nest boxes when I lived in Oklahoma.

Swallows

Tree swallows are widespread across most of North America during the breeding season. They are most common in open areas near water. Wooded swamps, lake shores, and parks near water make ideal tree swallow habitat. In the fall, tree swallows migrate in huge flocks to the southern United States and to Mexico.

Though not as social as purple martins, which nest communally in the familiar white apartment houses, tree swallows will tolerate close neighbors. If nest boxes are placed every 30 to 40 feet in suitable habitat, it is not unusual for most of the boxes to be occupied. Biologists call these breeding groups loose colonies.

In some places, folks regard tree swallows as pests because they compete with bluebirds for nest sites. Bluebird boxes are the perfect size for use by tree swallows. However, because tree swallows are single-brooded and bluebirds nest two—and sometimes three times—per year, this competition usually lasts only through the first nesting cycle. This competition can be avoided entirely by offering bluebird boxes in pairs, spaced about 10 feet apart. Bluebirds will take one box and tree swallows the other. The swallows will defend both boxes from others of their species.

BILL THOMPSON, III

Tree swallows will readily use nest boxes placed in appropriate habitat.

Tree swallow nests are among the easiest to recognize. The female lays 4 to 6 pure white eggs in a simple, grassy cup lined with feathers, often white chicken or duck feathers. She then incubates them for 13 to 16 days. Depending on weather and the availability of food, the young swallows may fledge 16 to 24 days after hatching. When food is abundant and the weather is warm, nestlings grow faster than when conditions are less favorable.

Violet-green swallows occur along the western third of North America from Alaska to Mexico. Their behavior and habits are similar to that of tree swallows, and where their ranges overlap, the two species often compete for cavities, though violet-greens seem to prefer the highest cavities available. Violet-greens also lay 4 or 5 white eggs in a feather-lined nest. Incubation by the female lasts about two weeks and the nestling stage is similar and also based upon weather and food abundance. Both tree and violet-green swallows are single-brooded.

Nest boxes intended for these swallows should be equipped inside with an escape ladder just below the hole. The ladder can be a series of horizontal cuts in the wood or a piece of screening or hardware cloth tacked to the inside front, below the hole. This ladder enables weak adults to escape the box early in the spring. Cold weather that occurs after the swallows return in the spring can send their food supply—flying insects—into hiding. If the swallows go without food for a few days, they get too weak to leave the box in which they've sheltered during the cold weather. When seasonal temperatures return, the ladder gives the swallows a foothold to climb out of the box for a crucial meal. Without the ladder, they sometimes starve in the box. Later in the nesting season, the ladder also provides an easy foothold for fledglings. (Note: When installing screen or hardware cloth, make sure that there is no space between the ladder material and the front wall of the box, where bird legs might get caught. Also, make sure the screen or cloth has no exposed sharp edges.)

The third common cavity-nesting swallow is the **purple martin**. Social apartment-dwellers, the purple martin's nesting cycle is longer than that of tree or violet-green swallows. The female martin lines her compartment with fresh green leaves atop a base of mud and small twigs, and lays a clutch of 4 to 6 eggs. She incubates them for 15 to 16 days. After hatching, nestlings remain in the nest for as long as 35 days.

Over the centuries, dating back to Native Americans, the purple martin's nesting preferences have evolved in close association with human beings. Consequently, purple martins have very specific preferences as to habitat, housing styles and sizes, and location. They prefer roomy nest cavities in open habitat, located within 100 feet of a human residence or structure. The most readily accepted martin housing is painted white and located near a body of water. In the eastern two-thirds of North America, purple martins are totally reliant upon human-supplied housing. In the martin's range west of the Rockies, however, natural cavities are the most regularly used nest sites.

If you are specifically interested in providing housing for purple martins, see *Enjoying Purple Martins More*, by Richard Wolinski, published by *BWD* Press. (See the back panel of this booklet for a description.)

Bluebirds

There is no doubt that the booming interest in nest boxes and cavity-nesting birds can be attributed to our three species of bluebirds.

For specific and in-depth information on providing housing for bluebirds, I refer you to another *BWD* Press booklet, *Enjoying Bluebirds More*, by Julie Zickefoose. This booklet is filled with valuable advice for the bluebird landlord. (See the back panel of this booklet for more information.)

Ideally a bluebird box should be mounted about 5 to 6 feet above the ground. It should be at least 50 feet from the nearest wooded area, though a few scattered trees nearby are acceptable. To minimize competitive squabbling with neighboring bluebirds, the next nearest nest box should be no closer than 100 yards.

Eastern bluebirds occur east of the Rocky Mountains in open country. Farmland, grazed pastures, large mowed lawns, and cemeteries provide ideal habitat—short grass with scattered trees. (Avoid encouraging bluebirds to nest in areas in which pesticide and herbicide use is intense.) Bluebirds typically raise two broods per year, though the farther south you live the more likely you are to observe three broods.

Eastern bluebird nests are simple, unlined cups fashioned from grasses or pine needles. Clutch size varies from 3 to 6 sky-blue eggs. First-year breeders usually have smaller clutches than experienced females, and in any given year, early nests usually have more eggs than later nests.

The female eastern bluebird normally incubates the eggs for 14 days. During cool, wet weather the eggs may require an extra day or two to hatch. In midsummer, when ambient temperatures are higher, the eggs may hatch in 12 days. The nestling period usually lasts 16 to 20 days, but varies. Under ideal conditions with abundant food, young bluebirds may fledge in 15 or 16 days. If food is in short supply, nestlings may grow more slowly and may remain in the nest for 22 or 23 days.

Western and **mountain bluebirds** occur in the western third of North America. Mountain bluebirds prefer higher elevations, generally above an altitude of 5,000 feet. Western bluebirds are commonly found at lower elevations. The nesting biology of western and mountain bluebirds differs little from that of eastern bluebirds, except for the number of broods per year. Western and mountain bluebirds are double-brooded, but at high elevations, mountain bluebirds raise only a single brood. If you are planning to provide nest boxes for mountain bluebirds, please consult

A female eastern bluebird inspects a nest box many times before nest building begins.

BILL THOMPSON, III

The ash-throated flycatcher, a western relative of the great crested flycatcher, is an enthusiastic user of nest boxes.

the chart at the end of this booklet before buying or building the housing. Mountain bluebirds have broader shoulders, and so require a slightly larger entrance hole (1 9/16 inches) than conventional bluebird houses offer (1½-inches). Their larger broods also call for a roomier nest box—a five-inch-square floor seems to work best.

Flycatchers

Though at least six species of flycatch-ers occasionally nest in cavities, only two are widely distributed. **Great crested flycatchers** inhabit forests east of the Rockies, and **ash-throated flycatchers** live in the chaparral, deserts, and dry woodlands of the Southwest. Both species migrate to Central America in winter, returning to North America to breed in the spring.

I have had little experience with great crested flycatchers, probably because most of my bluebird-sized nest boxes would be a tight fit for them.

Like most birds, great crested flycatchers renest if their first attempt fails.

The foundation of a great crested flycatcher's nest consists mostly of grasses, some twigs, and a few bits of moss. A feather or two sometimes decorates the rim of the cup. Almost always lining the cup, and sometimes trailing out the nest hole, is the shed skin of a very large snake. Great crested flycatchers often place the cast-off skin of a mortal enemy in their nests. The reasons are unclear, but it is believed to serve to discourage other cavity nesters from competing for that particular nest site.

A single clutch of five eggs is typical for great crested flycatchers. The female incubates the clutch for two weeks. The nestling period varies from 14 to 21 days depending on food availability.

In southern Arizona and South Texas, the **brown-crested flycatcher** (formerly called Wied's flycatcher) occupies the great crested flycatcher niche, while across a much larger portion of the Southwest the ash-throated flycatcher plays the part. Their nesting biology differs little from the great crested's. Ash-throated flycatchers use a variety of humanmade objects as nest sites, including mailboxes, drain pipes, and exhaust pipes, so they should be easy to attract with a suitable nest box in suitable habitat.

Warblers

Only two North American warblers nest in cavities. One occurs in the East, the other in the West.

The **prothonotary warbler** lurks among dark, wooded swamps and waterways throughout much of the East. Although it is more common in the southern half of its range, prothonotaries can be found as far north as Erie, Pennsylvania, and northern New Jersey.

After the male selects the cavity, the female prothonotary builds the nest. She then lays a clutch of 4 to 6 eggs. Incubation, conducted by the female alone, lasts about 13 days. Southern pairs raise two broods per year; northern prothonotaries are single-brooded.

Lucy's warbler lives along watercourses in mesquite, willow, and cottonwood thickets in west Texas and the southern portions of New Mexico, Arizona, and California. The male is a tiny gray ghost of a bird with a rusty crown and rump.

The female builds the nest and lays 4 or 5 eggs. Not much is known about the nesting biology of the Lucy's warbler. I've also found no assertions that Lucy's warblers use nest boxes, though I suspect that they would if boxes were available.

Hawks and Owls

It comes as a surprise to many people, but cavity-nesting raptors are among the easiest birds to attract to nest boxes. Kestrels and screech-owls, in particular, are widespread and relatively common. The drawback is that these raptors eat birds as well as small mammals and insects. Kestrels, for example, prefer open country just like bluebirds. Erecting nest boxes for both might seem self-defeating, but remember that bluebirds are just one of many in the array of kestrel prey.

I've found that **American kestrels** are the easiest of all cavity nesters to attract to nest boxes. In suitable habitat, put up a large box, 8 inches by 8 inches by 18 inches high with a three-inch hole, and you'll get kestrels. And if you live on or near a farm you'll soon notice fewer starlings, house sparrows, and cowbirds. Like most predators, kestrels take the most common prey available.

Kestrels are the smallest and most common falcon in North America.

They occur in open country—hayfields, pastures, orchards, rangeland, desert—all across the continent. They often perch on power lines, watching the ground below for grasshoppers, small snakes, and small birds. Sometimes they hover 20 to 30 feet above the ground, waiting for a mouse to get careless.

Kestrels incubate their eggs for about 30 days. The young remain in the cavity for another 30 days. For about two weeks after the young leave the nest, the adults continue to feed them. At night the fledglings return to the nest cavity with the female.

Parent kestrels teach their young to hunt and feed by example. They speed the weaning process by withholding food. As the adults reduce their attention to their offspring, the young quickly learn to fend for themselves.

If you live in a wooded setting, you will have better luck attracting screech-owls than kestrels. One of the reasons screech-owls are easy to attract to nest boxes is that they use them all year long for several different purposes.

Screech-owls live in woodlots throughout the United States, but they're rarely seen because they are strictly nocturnal. **Eastern screech-owls** occur east of the Rockies; **western screech-owls** live west of these mountains. I often hear eastern screech-owls in our woods when I step outside for a late night breath of

American kestrels, such as this female, prefer large nest boxes placed near open habitat.

fresh air. Their tremulous whinny is as distinctive as it is eerie.

Screech-owls use cavities or nest boxes throughout the year. They nest in them in the spring, and they use cavities as a protected place to eat prey and as a roost during other times.

In the fall, after most deciduous trees have lost their leaves, screech-owls will enter cavities to consume their prey.

There are a number of reasons for this. First of all, eating in a protected dining area is safer than eating on an exposed perch. A hungry screech-owl busy eating a mouse is, in turn, easy prey for a great horned owl in the open woods. Secondly, the cavity can serve as a storage area for any uneaten prey items, or as a food-caching spot for use during extended periods of bad weather.

Screech-owls are small, only about 8 or 9 inches tall.

There are some telltale signs that may help you to know if an owl is using your nest box. The box and the ground directly beneath it may be littered with regurgitated owl pellets. Owls swallow their prey whole. They digest all but the skulls, bones, fur, and feathers of the rodents and birds that make up the bulk of their diet. These indigestible parts are regurgitated in the form of hard pellets. Biologists can tell what owls eat by dissecting these pellets and studying their contents.

If screech-owls nest in one of your nest boxes, you can expect to find 4 or 5 nearly round white eggs. Incubation takes about 26 days, but unlike many birds, owls do not wait until all the eggs are laid to begin incubating. Often owls begin incubating after the first or second egg is laid. The practical result is that the eggs hatch in the order they were laid. Consequently owl nests often contain young of various ages.

In years when prey is abundant, all the owlets can survive. If food is scarce, the older, larger nestlings will outcompete their younger, smaller siblings. This natural balancing system allows the owls to have large broods when times are good.

In some parts of the country, other owls also use nest boxes. Northern saw-whet owls, which live in dense coniferous forests and wooded swamps across much of North America, often use nest boxes. Across Canada's northern forests, boreal owls inhabit dense forests and bogs. From the Rockies westward, northern pygmy

A red phase eastern screech-owl roosting inside a nest box.

MASLOWSKI WILDLIFE PRODUCTIONS

and flammulated owls are likely nest box candidates. And barn, barred, and even great horned owls may reward anyone willing to build and erect large, heavy boxes or nesting platforms. (See the reference charts at the end of this booklet for specifications.)

Ducks

Whenever I write about providing nest boxes for wildlife, many readers are surprised to find ducks, especially the spectacularly beautiful **wood duck**, on the list of cavity nesters. But wood ducks are just one of several common cavity-nesting North American ducks.

Ideal Nest Boxes for Wood Ducks

Wood ducks prefer large, deep nest boxes placed on poles or trees above or near water. One advantage of placing duck boxes over water is that the location makes for safer fledging for young ducks. (More on this later.)

To soften the bottom of the box, place a few handfuls of dry wood chips inside the box. The female wood duck will use these as a foundation for her nest. (Consult the reference chart on pages 32-33 for the proper dimensions of a wood duck box.)

Another feature of a wood duck box that can make a big difference for nestlings is an inside ladder. Tack a six-inch-wide strip of ¼-inch hardware cloth below the entrance hole on the inside. The ducklings use this to exit the nest box. Some duck boxes are designed with a front panel that slopes downward from the hole to the floor. This adaptation simulates a natural cavity and also makes it easier for ducks and ducklings to exit the box.

By March, most female woodies have mates, and the search for nest sites begins. Hens initiate the search and select the cavity. Within days, the female

MASLOWSKI WILDLIFE PRODUCTIONS

This male wood duck stands atop a potential nest site.

begins laying eggs. A typical clutch of 12 eggs is cradled in the debris at the bottom of the cavity (wood chips in a nest box). Toward the end of the egg-laying cycle, the hen may pluck some of her own down feathers and add them to the nest. After an incubation period of about 30 days, the eggs hatch. The drake has abandoned the hen by this time, and she rears the brood alone.

A few hours after the ducklings' first sunrise, the hen leaves the cavity and calls to the ducklings to follow her. They respond immediately by peeping and then jumping up toward the cavity's hole. Clinging to the cavity wall with strong legs and claws, the ducklings gradually work their way up to the hole. (Note: notches carved on the box's inside front panel help ducklings get a good grip.) Then, in what is truly a sight to behold, the ducklings jump to the ground or water below. Although natural cavities may be as high as 60 feet, the ducklings' small size and downy covering lets them land softly and unharmed.

As soon as the entire brood is on the ground, it follows the hen to the brood pond. Weak ducklings that can't make their way out of the cavity are left behind. If the nest is some distance from the brood pond, the overland trip to water can be hazardous. The longer the journey, the greater the odds are that a raccoon, hawk, or snake will snatch some or all of the brood. That's why it's best to put wood duck nest boxes directly over the water. Even in the water, ducklings face constant danger from unseen predators below—snapping turtles, large fish, and water snakes.

Other Ducks That Use Nest Boxes

Across the boreal forest of Canada, **common goldeneyes**, **common mergansers**, and **buffleheads** are cavity nesters that will use nest boxes. Along the Pacific Coast, from northern California to Alaska, **Barrow's goldeneye** can be added to the nest box list. And throughout much of the East and in some parts of the boreal North, **hooded mergansers** compete for nest boxes. In South Texas and southern Arizona, the **black-bellied whistling duck** nests in tree cavities in woodlands, though not always near water. These birds will readily accept nest boxes, lined with wood chips, within their breeding range.

Woodpeckers

Though woodpeckers create many of the natural cavities that other birds use, they themselves infrequently use nest boxes. That's because the act of excavating a cavity is an important part of a woodpecker's breeding behavior. Occasionally, some woodpeckers—especially flickers—use artificial cavities for nesting. There is one thing you can do to make a nest box attractive to woodpeckers, while saving the "hammerheads" a lot of time and effort. Stuff woodpecker boxes full of wood chips and pack them in firmly. Now a woodpecker can "excavate" a cavity in short order and still use a nest box. Among the species that sometimes use nest boxes are downy, hairy, golden-fronted, pileated, red-headed, Nuttall's, and red-bellied woodpeckers, and, of course, northern flickers.

One way to tell if woodpeckers are interested in using one of your nest boxes (especially one not filled with woodchips) is to examine the entrance holes for signs of enlargement. Woodpeckers, in their zeal to begin the nesting process, may sometimes enlarge the hole on a wooden bluebird or swallow house.

MASLOWSKI WILDLIFE PRODUCTIONS

Cavity excavation is an important part of courtship for woodpeckers such as this red-headed woodpecker.

House Sparrows and Starlings

No discussion of cavity nesters would be complete without some mention of house sparrows and starlings. These birds, both Old World natives, were introduced to North America in the mid-to-late 1800s. They flourished and can now be found all across North America. Unfortunately, they are both aggressive cavity nesters that routinely outcompete native species for nest sites. Often starlings and house sparrows kill an incubating adult of species such as bluebirds, swallows, and martins, and build their nests on top of the carcass.

Starlings are the easier-to-deal-with of the two—they can be excluded from basic bluebird nest boxes by limiting the entrance hole size. Starlings are simply too husky to fit through a 1½-inch-diameter entrance.

House sparrows, on the other hand, can squeeze through one-inch holes, which makes the house sparrow the bane of many nest box landlords. Lose one chickadee or a clutch of eggs to a house sparrow, and you'll understand this problem all too clearly.

Recognizing Starlings and House Sparrows and Their Nests

Starlings are mid-sized, all-dark birds with long, narrow, yellow bills. Because this species is so hardy, the starling may choose to breed at any time of year. Starling nests are messy affairs of grass, twigs, and sometimes even trash. These birds are loud and vociferous, and the nestlings are equally noisy before fledging.

House sparrows are members of the weaver finch family, and as such, they build large, bulky nests from grasses and weed stems. These nests often appear to have an overhanging roof, built up

the back of a nest box. House sparrows prefer roominess over any other attribute. Some bluebird trail operators are experimenting by limiting the interior space of bluebird houses to the point at which house sparrows won't attempt to use them, but at which bluebirds still can nest successfully in them.

If you live near an area where livestock are fed, you may find all your nest boxes taken over by house sparrows, which prefer to live near a source of grain. If this is the case, consider moving your nest boxes farther from the sparrows' food source.

Neither the starling nor the house sparrow is protected by federal or state law, so you may control these pests in any way you see fit, if you prefer direct action. However, you must be certain of the identity of any species nesting in your nest boxes before you resort to lethal control methods—all native North American bird species are protected by federal law. Another competitor control method is simply to be more persistent than the birds are. Remove newly built starling or sparrow nests every day, until the birds give up and look elsewhere to nest. This little game can go on for weeks, but in the long run, it's worth it.

Nest boxes provide a means of personal involvement in bird conservation. Natural cavities are in short supply in many areas, so without your efforts, many birds might not otherwise be able to nest and reproduce. Through the triumphs and tragedies of being a landlord to the birds you will experience nature's heartbeat, and perhaps gain a deeper understanding of the complex web of life. ➴

SPECIES	Interior Floor Size of Box (inches)	Interior Height of Box (inches)	Entrance Hole Diameter (inches)	Mount Box this High (feet)
Chickadees	4x4	9–12	$1^1/_8$–$1^1/_2$	5–15
Prothonotary & Lucy's warbler	4x4	12	$1^1/_4$	5–12
Titmice	4x4	12	$1^1/_2$	5–12
White-breasted Nuthatches	4x4	12	$1^1/_2$	5–12
Carolina Wrens	4x4	9–12	1–$1^1/_2$	5–10
Eastern Bluebird	4x4	12	$1^1/_2$	5–6
Western Bluebird	5x5	12	$1^1/_2$–$1^9/_{16}$	5–6
Mountain Bluebird	5x5	12	$1^9/_{16}$	5–6
Tree Swallow	5x5	10–12	$1^1/_2$	5–10
Violet-green Swallow	5x5	10–12	$1^1/_2$	5–10
Purple Martin	6x6	6	$2^1/_8$	15–25
Great-crested Flycatcher	6x6	12	$1^3/_4$–2	6–20
Ash-throated Flycatcher	6x6	12	$1^3/_4$–2	6–20
House Finch	5x5	10	$1^1/_2$	5–10
Downy Woodpecker	4x4	12	$1^1/_2$	5–20
Hairy Woodpecker	6x6	14	$1^1/_2$	8–20
Red-bellied Woodpecker	6x6	14	2	8–20
Golden-fronted Woodpecker	6x6	14	2	8–20
Red-headed Woodpecker	6x6	14	2	8–20
Northern Flicker	7x7	16–24	$2^1/_2$	10–20
Pileated Woodpecker	12x12	24	4	15–25
Bufflehead	7x7	17	3	5–15
Wood Duck	12x12	24	3x4	5–20
Hooded Merganser	12x12	24	3x4	5–30
Goldeneyes	12x12	24	$3^1/_4$ x $4^1/_4$	15–20
Common Merganser	12x12	24	5x6	8–20
Saw-whet Owl	7x7	12	$2^1/_2$	8–20
Screech-owls	8x8	18	3	8–30
Boreal Owl	8x8	18	3	8–30
Barred Owl	14x14	28	8	15–30
Barn Owl	12x36	16	6x7	15–30
American Kestrel	9x9	16–18	3	12–30

FOR ALL NEST BOXES: Interior height listed above refers to inside back panel.
Always baffle nest boxes. Sizes above are minimum ideal sizes for each species.
FOR WREN BOXES: Larger, oblong holes make it easier to get twigs into box.
FOR SWALLOW BOXES: Carve grooves, or place hardware cloth on inside of front of box.
FOR PURPLE MARTINS: Size listed here is for one compartment in a multi-unit martin house.
See *Enjoying Purple Martins More*.